BUSINESS CASE FOR AI:
WHY EVERY
BUSINESS NEEDS AN
AI
STRATEGY

I0416220

HENRY E. PARKINS

COPYRIGHT PAGE

TABLE OF CONTENTS

BUSINESS CASE FOR AI: WHY EVERY BUSINESS NEEDSAN AI STRATEGY

INTRODUCTION

In the rapidly evolving landscape of modern business, one phrase has emerged as both a buzzword and a beacon of transformation: Artificial Intelligence, or AI. From enhancing efficiency to driving innovation, AI has become the cornerstone of competitive advantage in nearly every sector. As businesses grapple with the challenges and opportunities of the digital age, the imperative to embrace AI has never been more pressing.

Welcome to "Business Case for AI: Why Every Business Needs an AI Strategy". In this book, we embark on a journey to explore the compelling reasons why AI isn't just a technological trend but a strategic imperative for businesses of all sizes and industries. As we delve into the depths of AI's impact and potential, we will uncover why developing an AI strategy is not only advisable but essential for long-term success.

The concept of AI, once relegated to the realm of science fiction, has now permeated every aspect of our lives. From virtual assistants streamlining our daily

7

tasks to predictive analytics revolutionizing industries, AI has transcended its roots to become an indispensable tool for driving growth and innovation. However, with great power comes great responsibility, and the ethical and practical considerations surrounding AI adoption cannot be understated.

In this book, we will navigate the complexities of AI, demystifying its underlying principles and exploring its myriad applications in the business world. We will examine case studies of organizations that have successfully integrated AI into their operations, learning valuable lessons from their triumphs and setbacks. From identifying use cases to mitigating risks, we will provide practical guidance for businesses embarking on their AI journey.

But beyond the practical implications, "Business Case for AI" is a call to action a manifesto for businesses to embrace the transformative potential of AI and chart a course towards a future of sustainable growth and innovation. We will explore not only the tangible benefits of AI but also the ethical considerations and societal impacts that accompany its widespread adoption.

As we embark on this exploration of the business case for AI, it is our hope that readers will come away inspired and informed, equipped with the knowledge and tools to navigate the complexities of the AI-driven economy. Whether you're a seasoned executive or an aspiring entrepreneur, the insights contained within these pages will empower you to harness the power of AI and propel your business towards greater heights of success.

Definition of AI

Artificial Intelligence (AI) refers to the simulation of human intelligence processes by computer systems. These processes include learning, reasoning, problem-solving, perception, and language understanding. AI technologies enable machines to perform tasks that traditionally required human intelligence, ranging from simple data analysis to complex decision-making.

At its core, AI seeks to replicate the cognitive abilities of humans, allowing machines to interpret and respond to data in ways that mimic human thought processes. This ability to analyze vast amounts of data and derive insights has made AI a transformative force across various industries, driving innovation, efficiency, and competitive advantage.

AI encompasses a diverse range of technologies, including machine learning, natural language processing, computer vision, robotics, and expert systems. These technologies enable machines to learn from experience, adapt to new inputs, and perform tasks with minimal human intervention.

In the context of business, AI holds the promise of revolutionizing operations, unlocking new opportunities, and driving growth. By leveraging AI technologies, businesses can automate routine tasks, optimize processes, personalize customer experiences, and uncover valuable insights from data.

However, it is essential to recognize that AI is not a panacea and comes with its own set of challenges and considerations. Ethical concerns, data privacy, bias in algorithms, and the impact on jobs are just a few of the issues that businesses must

10

navigate when integrating AI into their operations.

Despite these challenges, the potential of AI to transform businesses and industries is undeniable. By understanding the capabilities and limitations of AI, businesses can develop strategic plans to harness its power effectively and drive sustainable growth in the digital age.

Importance of AI in the Modern Business Landscape

In the dynamic and fast-paced modern business landscape, the importance of Artificial Intelligence (AI) cannot be overstated. As technology continues to advance at an unprecedented rate, businesses are faced with a myriad of challenges and opportunities, from changing consumer behaviors to evolving market dynamics. In this environment, AI emerges as a catalyst for innovation, efficiency, and strategic advantage.

Enhanced Decision-Making: In an era characterized by data abundance, AI empowers businesses to make more informed and timely decisions. By

analyzing vast volumes of structured and unstructured data, AI algorithms can uncover patterns, trends, and insights that human analysts may overlook. This capability enables executives to make data-driven decisions that are grounded in evidence and predictive analytics, rather than relying solely on intuition or past experience.

Improved Operational Efficiency:

AI technologies have the potential to streamline and automate repetitive tasks, reducing operational costs and freeing up human resources for more strategic endeavors. From automating customer service interactions to optimizing supply chain logistics, AI-driven solutions can enhance efficiency across various business functions, enabling organizations to operate more effectively in today's competitive landscape.

Personalized Customer Experiences: In an increasingly

personalized economy, AI enables businesses to deliver tailored experiences to individual customers at scale. Through techniques such as machine learning and natural language processing, AI algorithms can analyze customer behavior, preferences, and interactions to anticipate needs and deliver personalized recommendations, content, and services. This level of personalization fosters customer loyalty, enhances brand engagement, and drives revenue growth.

Innovation and Competitive Advantage:
In addition to optimizing existing processes, AI fuels innovation and drives competitive advantage by enabling businesses to explore new frontiers and disrupt traditional business models. From developing new products and services to reimagining customer experiences, AI unlocks a world of possibilities for forward-thinking organizations that are willing to embrace change and experiment with emerging technologies.

Agility and Adaptability:
In today's volatile and uncertain business environment, agility and adaptability are essential traits for survival and success. AI enables businesses to adapt to changing market conditions, consumer preferences, and competitive pressures by providing

13

real-time insights and predictive analytics. By leveraging AI-driven solutions, businesses can anticipate market shifts, identify emerging trends, and pivot their strategies accordingly, thereby maintaining a competitive edge in a rapidly evolving landscape.

In summary, the importance of AI in the modern business landscape cannot be overstated. From enhancing decision-making and improving operational efficiency to delivering personalized customer experiences and driving innovation, AI is reshaping the way businesses operate, compete, and thrive in the digital age. As businesses navigate the complexities of the AI-driven economy, developing a strategic approach to AI adoption becomes imperative, laying the foundation for sustainable growth and success in the years to come.

Overview

"Business Case for AI: Why Every Business Needs an AI Strategy" is a comprehensive guide that illuminates the transformative power of Artificial Intelligence (AI) in the modern business landscape. Grounded in practical insights and real-world examples, this book is designed to equip business leaders, executives, and entrepreneurs with the knowledge and tools needed to navigate the complexities of the AI-driven economy and develop effective strategies for success.

Objectives:

Educate Readers: The primary objective of this book is to educate readers about the importance of AI in the modern business landscape. By providing a clear understanding of AI concepts, technologies, and applications, readers will gain the knowledge needed to appreciate the transformative potential of AI and its implications for business strategy.

Make the Case for AI Adoption: Through compelling arguments and real-world examples, this book makes the case for why every business needs an AI strategy. By exploring the tangible benefits of AI adoption, from enhanced decision-making to improved operational efficiency, readers will gain insights into how AI can

drive innovation, competitiveness, and growth across various industries.

Provide Practical Guidance:

Recognizing the challenges and complexities of AI adoption, this book provides practical guidance for businesses seeking to develop AI strategies. From assessing organizational readiness to identifying use cases and mitigating risks, readers will learn actionable strategies and best practices for integrating AI into their operations effectively.

Foster Ethical and Responsible AI Practices:

In addition to exploring the potential benefits of AI, this book also addresses the ethical considerations and societal impacts of AI adoption. By fostering discussions around responsible AI practices, data privacy, bias mitigation, and algorithmic transparency, readers will gain insights into how businesses can harness the power of AI while upholding ethical standards and societal values.

Structure

Introduction: The book begins with an introduction to the transformative power of

16

AI and outlines the objectives and structure of the book.

Understanding AI: The second section provides an overview of AI concepts, technologies, and applications, laying the foundation for deeper exploration.

The Role of AI in Business: This section explores the importance of AI in driving innovation, competitiveness, and growth across various business functions and industries.

Challenges and Opportunities: The fourth section examines the challenges and opportunities associated with AI adoption, from ethical considerations to emerging trends and future outlook.

Building an AI Strategy: In this section, readers learn practical strategies and best practices for developing and implementing AI strategies tailored to their business objectives and organizational capabilities.

Case Studies: The book features case studies of organizations that have successfully integrated AI into their operations, highlighting key lessons learned and best practices.

Risks and Mitigation Strategies: This section explores the risks and challenges of AI adoption and provides strategies for mitigating risks and building trust in AI-driven systems.

Future Trends and Predictions: The final section explores emerging trends and predictions shaping the future of AI and its implications for businesses and society.

Conclusion: The book concludes with a recap of key insights and a call to action for businesses to embrace the transformative potential of AI and develop strategic approaches to AI adoption.

"Business Case for AI: Why Every Business Needs an AI Strategy" is a roadmap for businesses seeking to harness the power of AI and navigate the complexities of the AI-driven economy. Through a blend of theory, practical guidance, and real-world

examples, this book empowers readers to embrace AI as a catalyst for innovation, growth, and competitive advantage in the digital age.

CHAPTER 1

UNDERSTANDING AI

Artificial Intelligence (AI) represents the pinnacle of human ingenuity in replicating cognitive functions typically associated with human intelligence in machines. At its core, AI seeks to enable machines to perceive their environment, reason about situations, learn from data, and make decisions in a manner that mimics human intelligence.

History and Evolution of AI:

AI has its roots in the 1950s when researchers began exploring the concept of creating machines capable of performing tasks that required human intelligence.

The field has evolved significantly over the decades, witnessing breakthroughs in areas such as machine learning, neural networks, natural language processing, computer vision, and robotics.

Key Concepts and Terminologies:

Machine Learning: A subset of AI that focuses on enabling machines to learn from data without being explicitly programmed.

Neural Networks: Computational models inspired by the structure and function of the human brain, used in tasks such as pattern recognition and classification.

Natural Language Processing (NLP): The ability of computers to understand, interpret, and generate human language.

Computer Vision: The field of AI that enables computers to interpret and understand visual information from the real world.

Robotics: The intersection of AI and engineering, focusing on the design, construction, and programming of robots to perform tasks autonomously.

Types of AI Technologies:

Narrow AI: Also known as Weak AI, this type of AI is designed to perform a specific task or a narrow range of tasks. Examples include virtual assistants, recommendation systems, and image recognition algorithms.

General AI: Also known as Strong AI, this type of AI aims to exhibit human-like intelligence across a wide range of tasks and contexts. General AI remains largely theoretical and is the subject of ongoing research and debate.

Artificial General Intelligence (AGI): A hypothetical form of AI that possesses the ability to understand, learn, and apply knowledge across different domains, akin to human intelligence.

Superintelligence: A concept referring to AI systems that surpass human intelligence in all aspects, potentially leading to transformative changes in society.

History and Evolution of AI

The history of Artificial Intelligence (AI) is a rich tapestry of scientific inquiry, technological innovation, and visionary breakthroughs that have shaped the modern world. Dating back to the mid-20th century, the quest to create machines capable of exhibiting human-like intelligence has captivated the imaginations of scientists, researchers, and entrepreneurs alike.

Foundations of AI (1950s-1960s):

The birth of AI can be traced to the seminal work of pioneers such as Alan Turing, John McCarthy, and Marvin Minsky in the 1950s.

Alan Turing proposed the Turing Test in 1950 as a measure of a machine's ability to exhibit intelligent behavior indistinguishable from that of a human.

John McCarthy is credited with coining the term "Artificial Intelligence" in 1956 and organizing the Dartmouth Conference, which is considered the founding event of the AI field.

During this era, AI research focused on symbolic reasoning, logic, and problem-solving using rule-based systems and expert systems.

The AI Winter (1970s-1980s):

Despite initial optimism, progress in AI research stagnated during the 1970s and 1980s, leading to a period known as the "AI Winter."

Challenges such as limited computing power, lack of data, and unrealistic expectations contributed to a decline in funding and interest in AI research.

However, research continued in areas such as knowledge representation, planning, and robotics, laying the groundwork for future advancements.

Resurgence and Practical Applications (1990s-Present):

The late 20th century witnessed a resurgence of interest in AI fueled by advances in computing power, algorithms, and data availability.

Machine learning emerged as a dominant paradigm in AI research, with techniques such as neural networks, genetic algorithms, and reinforcement learning gaining prominence.

Practical applications of AI began to emerge across various domains, including natural language processing, computer vision, robotics, and expert systems.

Breakthroughs in areas such as deep learning, fueled by the availability of large datasets and scalable computing infrastructure, revolutionized AI research and paved the way for transformative applications in industry.

Current Landscape and Future Directions:

In the 21st century, AI has become ubiquitous, permeating every aspect of society and reshaping industries ranging from healthcare and finance to transportation and entertainment.

Advancements in AI technologies such as deep learning, reinforcement learning, and natural language processing continue to drive innovation and unlock new possibilities.

Ethical considerations, including bias in algorithms, data privacy, and the impact on jobs and society, have emerged as critical concerns that require careful attention and regulation.

Looking ahead, the future of AI promises even greater advancements, with the potential to revolutionize how we work, live, and interact with the world around us.

Key Concepts and Terminologies

Machine Learning (ML):

Machine learning is a subset of artificial intelligence that focuses on enabling machines to learn from data without being explicitly programmed.

ML algorithms identify patterns, trends, and insights within datasets, allowing machines to make predictions or decisions based on the information learned.

Neural Networks:

Neural networks are computational models inspired by the structure and function of the human brain.

They consist of interconnected nodes, or neurons, organized into layers, including input, hidden, and output layers.

Neural networks are capable of learning complex patterns and relationships within data, making them well-suited for tasks such as image recognition, natural language processing, and predictive modeling.

Natural Language Processing (NLP):

Natural language processing is the field of artificial intelligence that focuses on enabling computers to understand, interpret, and generate human language.

NLP algorithms analyze and process text data, enabling tasks such as sentiment analysis, text summarization, and language translation.

Computer Vision:

Computer vision is the field of artificial intelligence that enables computers to interpret and understand visual information from the real world.

Computer vision algorithms analyze images and videos, allowing machines to recognize objects, detect patterns, and extract meaningful information from visual data.

Deep Learning:

Deep learning is a subset of machine learning that focuses on training deep neural networks with multiple layers.

Deep learning algorithms learn hierarchical representations of data, enabling them to capture complex patterns and relationships within large datasets.

Deep learning has fueled breakthroughs in areas such as image recognition, speech recognition, and autonomous driving.

Reinforcement Learning:

Reinforcement learning is a type of machine learning that focuses on enabling agents to learn through trial and error.

In reinforcement learning, agents interact with an environment and learn to maximize rewards by taking actions that lead to desirable outcomes.

Reinforcement learning has applications in areas such as robotics, game playing, and autonomous systems.

Algorithm Bias:

Algorithm bias refers to systematic errors or inaccuracies in AI algorithms that result in unfair or discriminatory outcomes.

Bias can arise from various sources, including biased training data, flawed algorithm design, or inappropriate use of AI systems.

Addressing algorithm bias is critical for ensuring fairness, transparency, and accountability in AI-driven decision-making processes.

Ethical AI:

Ethical AI refers to the responsible development, deployment, and use of artificial intelligence systems that align with ethical principles and societal values.

Ethical AI considerations include issues such as fairness, transparency, accountability, privacy, and the impact on individuals and communities.

Businesses must prioritize ethical AI practices to build trust with customers, stakeholders, and society at large.

Types of AI Technologies

Narrow AI (Weak AI):

Narrow AI, also known as Weak AI, refers to artificial intelligence systems that are designed to perform a specific task or a narrow range of tasks.

Examples of narrow AI applications include virtual assistants like Siri and Alexa, recommendation systems used by streaming platforms, and image recognition algorithms employed in social media platforms.

General AI (Strong AI):

General AI, also known as Strong AI, is the hypothetical goal of creating artificial intelligence systems that possess the ability to understand, learn, and apply knowledge across a wide range of tasks and contexts.

Unlike narrow AI, which is task-specific, general AI would exhibit human-like intelligence and adaptability, enabling it to perform a broad spectrum of cognitive tasks.

General AI remains largely theoretical and is the subject of ongoing research and debate within the AI community.

Artificial General Intelligence (AGI):

Artificial General Intelligence (AGI) refers to the pursuit of creating AI systems that possess human-like intelligence and capabilities across multiple domains.

AGI aims to develop AI systems capable of reasoning, learning, problem-solving, and

30

adapting to new environments and tasks in a manner comparable to human intelligence.

While AGI remains a long-term goal, researchers continue to explore fundamental principles and techniques that may one day lead to its realization.

Superintelligence:

Superintelligence is a concept that describes AI systems that surpass human intelligence in all aspects.

Superintelligent AI would possess cognitive abilities far beyond those of the most brilliant human minds, enabling it to solve complex problems, make groundbreaking discoveries, and outperform humans in virtually every intellectual endeavor.

The prospect of superintelligence raises profound questions and concerns about the potential impact on society, ethics, and the future of humanity.

Applied AI Technologies:

Applied AI technologies encompass a diverse range of AI applications and tools that address specific business needs and objectives.

Examples of applied AI technologies include machine learning algorithms used for predictive analytics, natural language processing systems employed in chatbots and virtual assistants, computer vision algorithms applied in image recognition and object detection, and robotics technologies used in automation and autonomous systems.

CHAPTER 2

THE ROLE OF AI IN BUSINESS

Artificial Intelligence (AI) has emerged as a transformative force in the modern business landscape, revolutionizing how organizations operate, innovate, and compete in today's digital economy. From enhancing efficiency to driving innovation, AI plays a multifaceted role in shaping the success and sustainability of businesses across industries. Understanding the pivotal role of AI in business is essential for organizations seeking to harness its power and unlock new opportunities for growth and competitiveness.

Enhancing Efficiency and Productivity:

AI enables businesses to automate repetitive tasks and streamline operations, enhancing efficiency and productivity across various functions.

Automation of manual processes, such as data entry, document processing, and customer service inquiries, allows

33

employees to focus on higher-value tasks that require human creativity and problem-solving skills.

AI-driven systems can optimize resource allocation, improve workflow management, and reduce operational costs, leading to increased efficiency and profitability for businesses.

Improving Decision-Making Processes:

AI empowers businesses to make data-driven decisions by analyzing large volumes of structured and unstructured data to uncover insights and trends.

Machine learning algorithms can identify patterns, correlations, and anomalies within datasets, enabling businesses to anticipate market trends, identify customer preferences, and mitigate risks.

Predictive analytics powered by AI can forecast demand, optimize pricing strategies, and personalize marketing campaigns, enabling businesses to make informed decisions that drive revenue growth and competitive advantage.

Enabling Innovation and Competitive Advantage:

AI fosters innovation by enabling businesses to develop new products, services, and business models that leverage advanced technologies and data-driven insights.

AI-powered technologies such as natural language processing, computer vision, and robotics enable businesses to create immersive customer experiences, personalized recommendations, and intelligent automation solutions.

By embracing AI-driven innovation, businesses can differentiate themselves in the marketplace, respond quickly to changing customer demands, and stay ahead of competitors in rapidly evolving industries.

Optimizing Customer Experiences:

AI enables businesses to deliver personalized and seamless customer experiences across various touchpoints, driving customer satisfaction and loyalty.

Natural language processing and sentiment analysis algorithms empower businesses to understand customer feedback, preferences, and behavior, enabling them to tailor products, services, and communications to individual needs.

AI-powered chatbots and virtual assistants provide real-time support and assistance to customers, improving response times, reducing friction, and enhancing overall satisfaction with the brand.

Driving Operational Excellence:

AI facilitates continuous improvement and optimization of business processes by analyzing data, identifying inefficiencies, and recommending actionable insights.

AI-driven predictive maintenance systems can anticipate equipment failures, optimize maintenance schedules, and minimize downtime, reducing costs and improving operational reliability.

Supply chain optimization powered by AI enables businesses to forecast demand, optimize inventory levels, and mitigate supply chain risks, ensuring timely delivery of products and services to customers.

In summary, the role of AI in business is multifaceted and far-reaching, encompassing efficiency gains, data-driven decision-making, innovation, customer experience optimization, and operational excellence. By embracing AI as a strategic imperative, businesses can unlock new opportunities for growth, competitiveness, and sustainability in the increasingly digital and AI-driven economy. The business case for AI is clear: every organization needs an AI strategy to thrive and succeed in the fast-paced and dynamic landscape of the 21st century.

Enhancing Efficiency and Productivity

In the dynamic and competitive landscape of modern business, efficiency and productivity are essential drivers of success. Businesses are constantly seeking ways to streamline operations, optimize processes, and maximize resource utilization to stay agile and responsive to changing market demands. In this context, Artificial Intelligence (AI) emerges as a powerful enabler, offering businesses innovative solutions to enhance efficiency and productivity across various functions and operations.

Automation of Repetitive Tasks:

AI enables businesses to automate routine and repetitive tasks that traditionally require human intervention, freeing up valuable time and resources for more strategic endeavors.

Tasks such as data entry, document processing, and administrative workflows can be automated using AI-powered systems, reducing manual errors, minimizing processing times, and increasing overall efficiency.

By automating repetitive tasks, businesses can optimize resource allocation, streamline operations, and focus human efforts on higher-value activities that require creativity, critical thinking, and problem-solving skills.

Optimization of Workflow Processes:

AI-driven workflow optimization tools analyze data and identify bottlenecks, inefficiencies, and areas for improvement within business processes and operations.

38

Machine learning algorithms can analyze historical data and patterns to predict future workflow performance, enabling businesses to proactively optimize resource allocation, prioritize tasks, and allocate resources more effectively.

By optimizing workflow processes, businesses can streamline operations, reduce cycle times, and improve overall productivity, leading to cost savings and increased competitiveness in the marketplace.

Personalized Task Management and Scheduling:

AI-powered task management and scheduling tools leverage machine learning algorithms to analyze individual work patterns, preferences, and priorities, enabling personalized task management and scheduling recommendations.

These tools can intelligently prioritize tasks, allocate resources, and schedule appointments based on factors such as deadlines, dependencies, and resource availability, optimizing time management and enhancing productivity.

By providing personalized task management and scheduling capabilities, AI enables employees to manage their workloads more effectively, reduce stress, and improve work-life balance, leading to higher levels of engagement and satisfaction.

Real-time Performance Monitoring and Feedback:

AI-driven performance monitoring and feedback systems continuously monitor key performance indicators (KPIs), analyze trends, and provide real-time feedback to employees and managers.

These systems can identify performance issues, deviations from targets, and areas for improvement, enabling proactive intervention and corrective action to maintain productivity and performance levels.

By providing real-time performance monitoring and feedback, AI empowers employees to track their progress, set goals, and make data-driven decisions to improve their performance and achieve business objectives more effectively.

40

Predictive Maintenance and Resource Allocation:

AI-powered predictive maintenance systems analyze historical data, sensor readings, and equipment performance metrics to predict and prevent equipment failures and downtime.

These systems can identify potential issues before they occur, schedule maintenance activities proactively, and optimize resource allocation to ensure optimal equipment performance and availability.

By implementing predictive maintenance and resource allocation strategies, businesses can minimize downtime, reduce maintenance costs, and maximize the lifespan of critical assets, enhancing operational efficiency and productivity.

In summary, AI offers businesses a multitude of opportunities to enhance efficiency and productivity by automating repetitive tasks, optimizing workflow processes, providing personalized task management and scheduling capabilities, enabling real-time performance monitoring and feedback, and implementing predictive maintenance and resource allocation strategies. By leveraging AI-driven solutions, businesses can streamline operations, improve resource utilization, and drive sustainable growth and competitiveness in the digital age. A strategic approach to AI adoption is essential for businesses seeking to unlock the full potential of AI and maximize its impact on efficiency and productivity across the organization.

Improving Decision-Making Processes

In the complex and fast-paced world of business, effective decision-making is critical for success. Organizations must navigate a myriad of factors, ranging from market trends and customer preferences to resource constraints and competitive pressures, to make informed decisions that drive growth and profitability. In this context, Artificial Intelligence (AI) emerges as a powerful tool for improving decision-making processes, enabling businesses to analyze data, uncover insights, and make strategic decisions with confidence and agility.

Data-driven Insights and Analysis:

AI enables businesses to analyze vast volumes of structured and unstructured data to uncover patterns, trends, and insights that may not be apparent through traditional analysis methods.

Machine learning algorithms can identify correlations, anomalies, and causal relationships within datasets, providing valuable insights into customer behavior, market dynamics, and operational performance.

By leveraging data-driven insights and analysis, businesses can make informed decisions based on evidence and empirical evidence, reducing uncertainty and mitigating risks associated with decision-making.

Predictive Analytics and Forecasting:

AI-powered predictive analytics algorithms use historical data and statistical modeling techniques to forecast future trends, outcomes, and probabilities.

43

These algorithms can predict customer demand, market fluctuations, and business performance metrics, enabling businesses to anticipate changes, plan proactively, and capitalize on emerging opportunities.

By leveraging predictive analytics and forecasting, businesses can optimize resource allocation, mitigate risks, and make strategic decisions that drive growth and competitive advantage in the marketplace.

Real-time Decision Support Systems:

AI-driven decision support systems provide real-time insights, recommendations, and alerts to help businesses make timely and informed decisions in rapidly changing environments.

These systems analyze streaming data, sensor readings, and external signals to identify patterns, detect anomalies, and surface relevant information to decision-makers.

By providing real-time decision support, AI empowers businesses to respond quickly to market dynamics, customer needs, and competitive threats, enabling agile and adaptive decision-making processes.

Optimization and Simulation Modeling:

AI enables businesses to optimize decision-making processes through simulation modeling, scenario analysis, and optimization techniques.

Simulation models simulate different scenarios, variables, and parameters to evaluate the potential impact of decisions on business outcomes, enabling businesses to assess risks and trade-offs before making decisions.

By leveraging optimization and simulation modeling, businesses can identify optimal strategies, allocate resources efficiently, and minimize costs while maximizing returns, enhancing decision-making effectiveness and performance.

Personalized and Context-aware Recommendations:

AI-powered recommendation systems leverage machine learning algorithms to analyze user preferences, behavior, and historical interactions to provide personalized and context-aware recommendations.

These systems can recommend products, services, and content tailored to individual preferences, increasing engagement, conversion rates, and customer satisfaction.

By delivering personalized and context-aware recommendations, AI enhances decision-making processes for both businesses and customers, driving revenue growth and loyalty in competitive markets.

In summary, AI offers businesses a multitude of opportunities to improve decision-making processes by providing data-driven insights and analysis, predictive analytics and forecasting, real-time decision support systems, optimization and simulation modeling, and personalized and context-aware recommendations. By leveraging AI-driven solutions, businesses can make informed decisions with confidence and agility, driving growth, innovation, and competitive advantage in the digital age. A strategic approach to AI adoption is essential for businesses seeking to unlock the full potential of AI and maximize its impact on

46

decision-making processes across the organization.

Enabling Innovation and Competitive Advantage

In today's rapidly evolving business landscape, innovation is the cornerstone of success. Businesses must continually adapt, evolve, and innovate to stay ahead of the competition, anticipate customer needs, and capitalize on emerging opportunities. Artificial Intelligence (AI) has emerged as a powerful catalyst for innovation, enabling businesses to reimagine processes, products, and services in ways that drive growth and sustain competitive advantage. Understanding how AI enables innovation and fosters competitive advantage is essential for businesses seeking to thrive in the digital age and capitalize on the transformative potential of AI-driven technologies.

Advanced Data Analytics and Insights:

AI enables businesses to analyze vast volumes of data to uncover valuable

47

insights, patterns, and trends that drive innovation and inform strategic decision-making.

Machine learning algorithms can identify correlations, anomalies, and hidden patterns within datasets, providing valuable insights into customer behavior, market dynamics, and emerging trends.

By leveraging advanced data analytics and insights, businesses can identify new opportunities, optimize processes, and make informed decisions that drive innovation and competitive advantage in the marketplace.

Product and Service Innovation:

AI empowers businesses to innovate and differentiate their products and services by leveraging advanced technologies such as natural language processing, computer vision, and predictive analytics.

Businesses can develop AI-powered products and services that deliver personalized experiences, anticipate customer needs, and provide intelligent recommendations, enhancing customer satisfaction and loyalty.

48

By incorporating AI-driven capabilities into their offerings, businesses can unlock new revenue streams, expand market reach, and create unique value propositions that set them apart from competitors.

Process Optimization and Automation:

AI enables businesses to optimize and automate processes across various functions and operations, driving efficiency, scalability, and cost savings.

Machine learning algorithms can automate routine tasks, streamline workflows, and reduce manual errors, freeing up human resources to focus on more strategic initiatives.

By embracing process optimization and automation, businesses can enhance productivity, accelerate time-to-market, and gain a competitive edge in rapidly evolving industries.

Customer Experience Enhancement:

AI enables businesses to deliver seamless, personalized, and engaging customer experiences across multiple touchpoints, driving satisfaction, loyalty, and retention.

Natural language processing and sentiment analysis algorithms can analyze customer feedback, preferences, and sentiment to tailor interactions and recommendations to individual needs.

By providing personalized and context-aware experiences, businesses can enhance brand loyalty, foster customer advocacy, and differentiate themselves in crowded markets.

Agile Decision-Making and Adaptability:

AI empowers businesses to make agile, data-driven decisions and adapt quickly to changing market conditions, customer preferences, and competitive dynamics.

Real-time analytics and predictive modeling enable businesses to anticipate trends, identify opportunities, and pivot strategies in response to evolving market demands.

By fostering a culture of innovation, experimentation, and continuous improvement, businesses can embrace change, seize opportunities, and drive sustainable growth in the digital age.

In summary, AI serves as a powerful enabler of innovation and competitive advantage, empowering businesses to leverage advanced data analytics and insights, drive product and service innovation, optimize processes and automation, enhance customer experiences, and make agile, data-driven decisions. By embracing AI-driven technologies and strategies, businesses can unlock new opportunities, drive growth, and position themselves for long-term success in the increasingly competitive and dynamic business landscape. A strategic approach to AI adoption is essential for businesses seeking to harness the transformative power of AI and capitalize on its potential to drive innovation and competitive advantage across the organization.

CHAPTER 3

CHALLENGES AND OPPORTUNITIES

As businesses embrace the transformative potential of Artificial Intelligence (AI), they encounter a myriad of challenges and opportunities that shape their AI strategies and adoption journeys. Understanding these challenges and opportunities is essential for businesses seeking to harness the power of AI effectively and navigate the complexities of the AI-driven economy.

Challenges:

Data Quality and Availability:

One of the primary challenges in AI adoption is the quality and availability of data. AI algorithms rely on large volumes of high-quality data to train models effectively and generate accurate predictions.

Businesses may face issues related to data silos, inconsistencies, biases, and privacy concerns, which can hinder the performance and reliability of AI systems.

Talent and Skills Gap:

The demand for AI talent, including data scientists, machine learning engineers, and AI researchers, far exceeds the supply, creating a significant talent and skills gap in the workforce.

Recruiting and retaining skilled AI professionals can be challenging for businesses, particularly in competitive talent markets where demand for AI expertise is high.

Ethical and Regulatory Considerations:

Ethical considerations surrounding AI, including bias, fairness, transparency, and accountability, present significant challenges for businesses.

Businesses must navigate complex regulatory landscapes, including data privacy regulations, algorithmic transparency requirements, and ethical guidelines, to ensure responsible AI deployment and compliance with legal and ethical standards.

Integration and Scalability:

Integrating AI solutions into existing IT infrastructures and business processes can be complex and challenging.

Businesses must consider factors such as interoperability, scalability, and compatibility with legacy systems when deploying AI solutions across the organization.

Risk Management and Security:

AI introduces new risks and security vulnerabilities that businesses must address, including data breaches, adversarial attacks, and algorithmic biases.

Businesses must implement robust risk management and cybersecurity measures to protect sensitive data, ensure algorithmic fairness, and mitigate the potential risks associated with AI adoption.

Opportunities:

Innovation and Differentiation:

AI enables businesses to innovate and differentiate themselves in the marketplace by developing AI-powered products, services, and business models.

54

By leveraging AI-driven technologies, businesses can create unique value propositions, enhance customer experiences, and gain a competitive edge in rapidly evolving industries.

Operational Efficiency and Cost Savings:

AI enables businesses to streamline operations, automate routine tasks, and optimize resource allocation, driving operational efficiency and cost savings.

By automating manual processes and reducing inefficiencies, businesses can improve productivity, accelerate time-to-market, and achieve greater agility in response to changing market dynamics.

Data-driven Insights and Decision-making:

AI empowers businesses to leverage data-driven insights and predictive analytics to make informed decisions and drive strategic initiatives.

By analyzing large volumes of data, identifying patterns, and predicting future trends, businesses can optimize decision-making processes, mitigate risks, and capitalize on emerging opportunities in the marketplace.

Enhanced Customer Experiences:

AI enables businesses to deliver personalized, context-aware, and seamless customer experiences across multiple touchpoints.

By leveraging AI-driven technologies such as natural language processing, computer vision, and recommendation systems, businesses can anticipate customer needs, tailor interactions, and foster customer loyalty and advocacy.

Strategic Partnerships and Ecosystem Collaboration:

AI presents opportunities for businesses to forge strategic partnerships and collaborate within ecosystems to drive innovation and scale AI initiatives.

By partnering with technology vendors, research institutions, and industry peers, businesses can access expertise, resources, and networks that accelerate AI adoption and create value for stakeholders.

In summary, while AI presents challenges and complexities for businesses, it also offers unprecedented opportunities for innovation, differentiation, efficiency, and growth. By addressing the challenges and embracing the opportunities presented by AI, businesses can develop strategic AI strategies that unlock new possibilities, drive sustainable competitive advantage, and position them for success in the digital age. A proactive and strategic approach to AI adoption is essential for businesses seeking to harness the full potential of AI and thrive in the increasingly AI-driven economy.

Ethical Considerations and Responsible AI Practices

As businesses harness the power of Artificial Intelligence (AI) to drive innovation, improve efficiency, and enhance customer experiences, they must also navigate a complex landscape of ethical considerations and responsibilities. In the pursuit of AI-driven solutions, businesses have a responsibility to ensure that their practices are ethical, transparent, and aligned with societal values. Understanding the ethical considerations and adopting responsible AI practices is essential for businesses

57

seeking to build trust, mitigate risks, and maximize the benefits of AI for both their stakeholders and society as a whole.

Algorithmic Bias and Fairness:

AI algorithms can inadvertently perpetuate biases present in training data, leading to discriminatory outcomes and unfair treatment of individuals or groups.

Businesses must proactively identify and mitigate algorithmic biases through rigorous testing, validation, and ongoing monitoring of AI systems.

Adopting fairness-aware algorithms, diverse training datasets, and transparent decision-making processes can help mitigate the risk of bias and promote fairness and equity in AI applications.

Transparency and Explainability:

Transparency and explainability are essential principles for fostering trust and accountability in AI-driven systems.

Businesses should strive to make AI algorithms and decision-making processes transparent and understandable to stakeholders, including customers, regulators, and employees.

Providing explanations for AI-driven decisions, disclosing data sources and algorithms, and promoting algorithmic transparency can help build trust and facilitate informed decision-making.

Privacy and Data Protection:

AI relies on vast amounts of data to train models and make predictions, raising concerns about privacy, data protection, and individual autonomy.

Businesses must adhere to data privacy regulations, such as the General Data Protection Regulation (GDPR) in Europe and the California Consumer Privacy Act (CCPA) in the United States, to protect the privacy and rights of individuals.

Implementing robust data governance frameworks, obtaining informed consent for data collection and processing, and anonymizing sensitive information can help mitigate privacy risks and ensure compliance with regulatory requirements.

Accountability and Governance:

Accountability and governance mechanisms are essential for ensuring responsible AI practices and mitigating risks associated with AI deployment.

59

Businesses should establish clear lines of accountability, designate responsible AI stewards, and establish governance structures to oversee AI initiatives and address ethical concerns.

Conducting regular audits, assessments, and impact analyses of AI systems, as well as fostering a culture of accountability and transparency, can help mitigate risks and ensure ethical AI practices across the organization.

Human-Centered Design and Empowerment:

Human-centered design principles emphasize the importance of designing AI systems that prioritize human well-being, autonomy, and empowerment.

Businesses should involve diverse stakeholders, including end-users, in the design, development, and deployment of AI-driven solutions to ensure that they meet user needs and preferences.

Empowering users with control over their data, providing opportunities for feedback and input, and promoting user-centric design principles can enhance trust, satisfaction, and acceptance of AI technologies.

Social Impact and Responsible Innovation:

AI has the potential to have profound social, economic, and environmental impacts, both positive and negative.

Businesses should consider the broader societal implications of their AI initiatives and strive to maximize positive outcomes while minimizing potential harms.

Engaging with stakeholders, conducting impact assessments, and incorporating ethical considerations into the design and implementation of AI solutions can help businesses mitigate risks and contribute to responsible innovation.

In summary, ethical considerations and responsible AI practices are integral to the success and sustainability of AI-driven initiatives. By prioritizing fairness, transparency, privacy, accountability, human-centered design, and social impact, businesses can build trust, foster innovation, and unlock the full potential of AI to create value for society and stakeholders. Embracing ethical AI

61

practices is not only a moral imperative but also a strategic imperative for businesses seeking to thrive in the increasingly complex and interconnected digital landscape.

Addressing Concerns about Job Displacement

As businesses embrace the transformative potential of Artificial Intelligence (AI), concerns about job displacement and workforce disruption have become increasingly prominent. While AI has the potential to automate routine tasks, optimize processes, and drive efficiency, it also raises legitimate concerns about the future of work and the impact on jobs, livelihoods, and communities. Addressing these concerns and proactively managing the transition to an AI-driven economy is essential for businesses seeking to build trust, foster resilience, and promote inclusive growth. Here are key strategies for addressing concerns about job displacement:

Reskilling and Upskilling Programs:

Businesses should invest in reskilling and upskilling programs to equip employees with the skills and competencies needed to thrive in an AI-driven workplace.

These programs should focus on developing critical thinking, problem-solving, creativity, and adaptability, as well as technical skills such as data analysis, programming, and AI literacy.

By investing in employee development and lifelong learning, businesses can empower workers to navigate technological changes, transition to new roles, and remain competitive in the labor market.

Transition Assistance and Support:

Businesses should provide transition assistance and support to employees affected by automation and AI-driven changes in the workforce.

This may include offering career counseling, job placement services, financial assistance, and retraining opportunities to help displaced workers transition to new roles or industries.

By demonstrating a commitment to employee well-being and job security, businesses can mitigate the negative impacts of job displacement and foster a culture of trust, loyalty, and resilience.

Job Redesign and Augmentation:

Rather than replacing human workers, AI can augment human capabilities and enhance job roles by automating routine tasks, enabling employees to focus on higher-value activities that require human judgment, creativity, and empathy.

Businesses should explore opportunities to redesign job roles, create new career pathways, and foster collaboration between humans and machines to maximize the potential of AI-driven technologies while preserving human dignity and purpose in the workplace.

Collaborative Workforce Planning and Stakeholder Engagement:

Businesses should engage in collaborative workforce planning and dialogue with employees, labor unions, government agencies, and other stakeholders to anticipate future labor market trends, identify skill gaps, and develop inclusive strategies for managing workforce transitions.

By fostering open communication, transparency, and stakeholder engagement, businesses can build consensus, address concerns, and co-create solutions that promote shared prosperity and economic resilience.

Investment in Social Safety Nets and Community Development:

Businesses should support investment in social safety nets, community development initiatives, and economic diversification efforts to mitigate the impact of job displacement and promote inclusive growth.

This may include advocating for policies that provide income support, healthcare, education, and retraining opportunities for displaced workers, as well as investing in community-based programs that foster entrepreneurship, innovation, and economic development.

In summary, addressing concerns about job displacement requires a multi-faceted and proactive approach that combines investment in reskilling and upskilling programs, transition assistance and support, job redesign and augmentation, collaborative workforce planning, and investment in social safety nets and community development. By prioritizing human-centered approaches to AI adoption and embracing responsible business practices, businesses can navigate the challenges of workforce disruption, build resilience, and unlock the full potential of AI to create shared prosperity and sustainable growth in the digital age.

Opportunities for New Business Models and Revenue Streams

Artificial Intelligence (AI) presents businesses with unprecedented opportunities to innovate, disrupt traditional business models, and unlock new sources of revenue. By leveraging AI-driven technologies and strategies, businesses can capitalize on emerging trends, meet evolving customer demands, and create value in innovative ways. Here are key opportunities for new business models and revenue streams enabled by AI:

Subscription-based AI Services:

Businesses can offer subscription-based AI services that provide access to AI-powered tools, platforms, and solutions on a recurring basis.

Subscription models enable businesses to generate predictable revenue streams, build long-term relationships with customers, and scale offerings to meet diverse needs and budgets.

AI-driven Predictive Analytics:

Businesses can monetize AI-driven predictive analytics by offering insights-as-a-service to customers across industries.

By leveraging advanced machine learning algorithms, businesses can analyze data, predict future trends, and provide actionable insights that enable customers to make informed decisions and drive business outcomes.

AI-powered Personalization and Recommendation Engines:

Businesses can monetize AI-powered personalization and recommendation engines by offering targeted advertising, product recommendations, and content curation services to consumers.

By leveraging machine learning algorithms to analyze user behavior, preferences, and interactions, businesses can deliver personalized experiences that enhance customer engagement and drive conversions.

68

AI-driven Automation and Process Optimization:

Businesses can monetize AI-driven automation and process optimization solutions by offering automation-as-a-service and workflow optimization services to enterprises.

By automating routine tasks, streamlining workflows, and optimizing resource allocation, businesses can help clients improve operational efficiency, reduce costs, and drive productivity gains.

AI-powered Customer Service and Support:

Businesses can monetize AI-powered customer service and support solutions by offering chatbots, virtual assistants, and conversational AI platforms to businesses across industries.

By leveraging natural language processing and machine learning algorithms, businesses can provide personalized, real-time support to customers, streamline interactions, and enhance customer satisfaction.

69

AI-driven Healthcare and Telemedicine Solutions:

Businesses can monetize AI-driven healthcare and telemedicine solutions by offering diagnostic tools, predictive analytics, and remote patient monitoring services to healthcare providers and patients.

By leveraging AI algorithms to analyze medical data, detect patterns, and predict health outcomes, businesses can improve patient care, optimize treatment plans, and reduce healthcare costs.

AI-powered Financial Services and Fintech Solutions:

Businesses can monetize AI-powered financial services and fintech solutions by offering predictive analytics, risk management, and algorithmic trading services to financial institutions and investors.

By leveraging AI algorithms to analyze market data, identify investment opportunities, and mitigate risks, businesses can help clients make data-driven decisions and achieve better financial outcomes.

AI-driven Supply Chain Optimization:

Businesses can monetize AI-driven supply chain optimization solutions by offering demand forecasting, inventory management, and logistics optimization services to manufacturers, retailers, and logistics providers.

By leveraging AI algorithms to analyze supply chain data, predict demand fluctuations, and optimize inventory levels, businesses can reduce costs, improve efficiency, and enhance supply chain resilience.

In summary, AI presents businesses with a wealth of opportunities to create new business models, unlock new revenue streams, and drive innovation across industries. By embracing AI-driven technologies and strategies, businesses can capitalize on emerging trends, address evolving customer needs, and stay ahead of the competition in the increasingly digital and AI-driven economy. A strategic approach to AI adoption is essential for

businesses seeking to harness the transformative potential of AI and maximize its impact on business growth and profitability.

CHAPTER 4

BUILDING AN AI STRATEGY

In today's rapidly evolving business landscape, Artificial Intelligence (AI) has emerged as a transformative force, offering businesses unprecedented opportunities to drive innovation, improve efficiency, and unlock new sources of value. However, harnessing the power of AI requires more than just adopting cutting-edge technologies it requires a strategic approach that aligns AI initiatives with business objectives, addresses organizational challenges, and maximizes the impact of AI across the entire enterprise. Here are key steps for building an effective AI strategy:

Define Business Objectives and Priorities:

Start by clearly defining your business objectives, priorities, and areas where AI can create the most value.

Identify specific use cases and business processes that can benefit from AI-driven

73

solutions, such as customer service optimization, predictive analytics, or supply chain management.

Assess Organizational Readiness and Capabilities:

Assess your organization's readiness and capabilities for AI adoption, including data infrastructure, technical expertise, and organizational culture.

Identify potential barriers to AI adoption, such as data silos, skills gaps, and resistance to change, and develop strategies to address these challenges.

Establish Clear Governance and Accountability:

Establish clear governance structures and accountability mechanisms to oversee AI initiatives and ensure alignment with business goals.

Define roles and responsibilities for key stakeholders, including executive sponsors, project managers, data scientists, and business users, to drive collaboration and accountability.

Develop a Data Strategy and Infrastructure:

Develop a comprehensive data strategy that addresses data collection, storage, quality, and governance requirements.

Invest in robust data infrastructure and analytics capabilities to support AI-driven initiatives, including data lakes, cloud platforms, and analytics tools.

Identify AI Technologies and Tools:

Identify the AI technologies and tools that best align with your business objectives and use case requirements.

Evaluate different AI platforms, frameworks, and solutions available in the market, considering factors such as scalability, interoperability, and ease of integration with existing systems.

Prioritize Ethical Considerations and Responsible AI Practices:

Prioritize ethical considerations and responsible AI practices throughout the AI lifecycle, from data collection and model development to deployment and monitoring.

Establish guidelines and frameworks for ethical AI development, including principles for fairness, transparency, accountability, and privacy protection.

Invest in Talent Development and Skills Acquisition:

Invest in talent development and skills acquisition to build a workforce with the technical expertise and domain knowledge needed to drive AI initiatives.

Provide training, certification programs, and learning opportunities to employees at all levels of the organization to enhance AI literacy and proficiency.

Pilot and Iterate AI Initiatives:

Start with small-scale pilots and proofs of concept to test AI-driven solutions in real-world scenarios and gather feedback from stakeholders.

Iterate and refine AI initiatives based on insights gained from pilot projects, incorporating lessons learned and best practices into future iterations.

Measure and Monitor Performance:

Define key performance indicators (KPIs) and metrics to measure the impact of AI initiatives on business outcomes, such as cost savings, revenue growth, and customer satisfaction.

Implement systems and processes for monitoring performance, tracking progress against targets, and making data-driven adjustments as needed.

Cultivate a Culture of Innovation and Continuous Improvement:

Foster a culture of innovation, experimentation, and continuous improvement to encourage exploration and adoption of new AI technologies and approaches.

Encourage collaboration, knowledge sharing, and cross-functional teamwork to drive innovation and overcome organizational silos.

In summary, building an AI strategy requires a holistic and structured approach that integrates business objectives, organizational capabilities, ethical considerations, and talent development. By following these key steps and embracing AI as a strategic imperative, businesses can unlock the full potential of AI to drive innovation, competitiveness, and sustainable growth in the digital age. A strategic AI strategy is not just about adopting technology—it's about transforming the way we work, innovate, and create value in a rapidly changing world.

Assessing Organizational Readiness for AI Adoption

Before embarking on the journey of Artificial Intelligence (AI) adoption, businesses must carefully assess their organizational readiness to ensure successful integration and maximize the benefits of AI-driven initiatives. Assessing organizational readiness involves evaluating various aspects of the organization, including its culture, capabilities, infrastructure, and leadership support. Here are key considerations for assessing organizational readiness for AI adoption:

Leadership Commitment and Vision:

Assess the level of leadership commitment and support for AI adoption across the organization, from the C-suite to middle management.

Evaluate whether leaders have a clear vision for how AI can create value, drive innovation, and achieve strategic objectives within the organization.

Culture and Change Readiness:

Evaluate the organization's culture and readiness for change, including its receptiveness to new technologies, experimentation, and risk-taking.

Assess whether employees are open to adopting AI-driven solutions, embracing new ways of working, and adapting to changes in job roles and responsibilities.

Technical Infrastructure and Data Capabilities:

Evaluate the organization's technical infrastructure and data capabilities to support AI adoption, including data storage, processing power, and analytics capabilities.

79

Assess the quality, quantity, and accessibility of data available within the organization, as well as data governance practices and data management processes.

Skills and Talent Availability:

Assess the organization's current workforce and talent pool to identify skills gaps and areas where additional expertise may be needed to support AI initiatives.

Evaluate whether the organization has the necessary talent in areas such as data science, machine learning, software development, and domain expertise relevant to AI applications.

Collaboration and Cross-functional Alignment:

Evaluate the level of collaboration and alignment across different departments, teams, and functions within the organization.

Assess whether there are existing channels for communication, knowledge sharing, and collaboration between technical and business stakeholders involved in AI initiatives.

Regulatory and Compliance Considerations:

Assess the organization's awareness of regulatory requirements and compliance considerations related to AI adoption, including data privacy, security, and ethical considerations.

Evaluate whether the organization has processes in place to ensure compliance with relevant regulations and guidelines governing AI deployment.

Resource Allocation and Budgetary Considerations:

Evaluate the organization's willingness and ability to allocate resources, including budget, time, and personnel, to support AI adoption and implementation efforts.

Assess whether there is sufficient funding, support, and buy-in from stakeholders to invest in AI initiatives and sustain long-term adoption and integration.

Risk Management and Contingency Planning:

Assess the organization's risk management practices and ability to identify, mitigate, and respond to potential risks and challenges associated with AI adoption.

Evaluate whether there are contingency plans and risk mitigation strategies in place to address issues such as data breaches, algorithmic biases, and technology failures.

In summary, assessing organizational readiness for AI adoption requires a comprehensive evaluation of leadership commitment, culture, technical infrastructure, skills and talent availability, collaboration, regulatory compliance, resource allocation, and risk management practices. By conducting a thorough assessment and addressing key areas of readiness, businesses can identify gaps, mitigate risks, and develop strategies to support successful AI adoption and integration across the organization. A proactive approach to assessing organizational readiness is essential for businesses seeking to harness the transformative potential of AI and drive sustainable growth and innovation in the digital age.

Identifying Use Cases and Business Objectives

Identifying use cases and business objectives is a crucial step in developing a comprehensive AI strategy that aligns with the needs and goals of the organization. By identifying specific use cases and business objectives for AI adoption, businesses can prioritize investments, allocate resources effectively, and maximize the impact of AI-driven initiatives. Here are key considerations for identifying use cases and business objectives for AI adoption:

Understand Business Challenges and Opportunities:

Begin by gaining a deep understanding of the organization's business challenges, pain points, and opportunities for improvement.

Conduct stakeholder interviews, workshops, and brainstorming sessions to identify areas where AI-driven solutions can address key business needs and create value.

Prioritize High-impact Areas:

Prioritize use cases and business objectives based on their potential impact on key performance metrics, strategic goals, and customer outcomes.

Focus on high-impact areas where AI can drive significant improvements in efficiency, effectiveness, revenue generation, cost reduction, or customer satisfaction.

Assess Feasibility and Complexity:

Assess the feasibility and complexity of potential use cases based on factors such as data availability, technical requirements, regulatory constraints, and organizational readiness.

Evaluate whether the organization has the necessary data, expertise, infrastructure, and resources to support AI-driven initiatives in identified use cases.

Consider Industry-specific Challenges and Trends:

Consider industry-specific challenges, trends, and opportunities that may impact the selection of use cases and business objectives for AI adoption.

Stay informed about emerging technologies, regulatory changes, and competitive dynamics within the industry to identify areas where AI can provide a competitive advantage or address industry-specific challenges.

Engage Cross-functional Stakeholders:

Engage cross-functional stakeholders, including business leaders, domain experts, data scientists, IT professionals, and end-users, in the process of identifying use cases and defining business objectives.

Foster collaboration and alignment between technical and business stakeholders to ensure that AI initiatives are closely aligned with organizational goals and priorities.

Define Clear Success Metrics:

Define clear success metrics and key performance indicators (KPIs) to measure the impact of AI-driven initiatives on business outcomes.

Identify quantifiable metrics that reflect the desired business objectives, such as revenue growth, cost savings, productivity gains, customer retention, or operational efficiency improvements.

Explore Innovative Opportunities:

Explore innovative opportunities for AI adoption that go beyond traditional use cases and business objectives.

Consider how AI can enable new business models, unlock untapped markets, or create entirely new products, services, or customer experiences that were not previously possible.

Iterate and Refine Use Cases Over Time:

Recognize that identifying use cases and business objectives is an iterative process that evolves over time.

Continuously evaluate and refine use cases based on feedback, insights, and changing business priorities to ensure that AI initiatives remain aligned with the organization's strategic direction.

In summary, identifying use cases and business objectives for AI adoption requires a strategic and collaborative approach that considers the organization's unique challenges, opportunities, and industry context. By prioritizing high-impact areas, engaging cross-functional stakeholders, defining clear success metrics, and exploring innovative opportunities, businesses can develop a robust AI strategy that drives tangible business value and positions the organization for long-term success in the digital age.

Developing a Roadmap for AI Implementation

Creating a roadmap for AI implementation is a critical step in translating strategic objectives into actionable plans and guiding the organization through the process of adopting and integrating AI-driven solutions. A well-defined roadmap helps align stakeholders, prioritize initiatives, allocate resources effectively, and manage the complexities of AI implementation. Here are key steps for developing a roadmap for AI implementation:

Define Strategic Objectives and Priorities:

Begin by clearly defining the organization's strategic objectives and priorities for AI adoption.

Align AI initiatives with business goals, customer needs, and industry trends to ensure that AI implementation efforts are closely tied to the organization's overall mission and vision.

Assess Current State and Identify Gaps:

Conduct a comprehensive assessment of the organization's current state of AI readiness, including technical capabilities, data infrastructure, skills, and organizational culture.

Identify gaps and areas of improvement that need to be addressed to support successful AI implementation and integration.

Set Clear Goals and Milestones:

Set clear, measurable goals and milestones for AI implementation, including timelines, deliverables, and success criteria.

Break down larger AI initiatives into smaller, manageable projects or phases to facilitate incremental progress and ensure alignment with strategic objectives.

Prioritize Use Cases and Initiatives:

Prioritize use cases and AI initiatives based on their potential impact, feasibility, complexity, and alignment with strategic priorities.

Consider factors such as business value, technical feasibility, data availability, and regulatory considerations when prioritizing AI implementation efforts.

Develop a Detailed Implementation Plan:

Develop a detailed implementation plan that outlines specific activities, tasks, and dependencies required to achieve the defined goals and milestones.

Define roles and responsibilities for key stakeholders, allocate resources, and establish timelines and deadlines for each phase of the implementation process.

Address Technical and Organizational Challenges:

Identify and address technical and organizational challenges that may impact AI implementation, such as data quality issues, skills gaps, and resistance to change.

Develop strategies to mitigate risks, overcome barriers, and foster a culture of innovation, collaboration, and continuous improvement within the organization.

Build Scalable and Sustainable Solutions:

Build scalable and sustainable AI solutions that can adapt to evolving business needs, technological advancements, and market dynamics over time.

Consider factors such as scalability, interoperability, security, and maintainability when designing and implementing AI-driven systems and architectures.

90

Establish Governance and Oversight Mechanisms:

Establish governance and oversight mechanisms to monitor progress, track performance against goals, and ensure accountability throughout the AI implementation process.

Define key performance indicators (KPIs), metrics, and reporting mechanisms to measure the impact of AI initiatives and make data-driven decisions.

Enable Continuous Learning and Improvement:

Foster a culture of continuous learning and improvement by encouraging experimentation, knowledge sharing, and feedback loops within the organization.

Encourage stakeholders to learn from successes and failures, iterate on solutions, and adapt strategies based on evolving business requirements and market dynamics.

Monitor and Evaluate Progress:

Continuously monitor and evaluate progress against the defined goals and milestones, making adjustments as needed

91

to stay on track and address emerging challenges.

Regularly review and update the AI implementation roadmap to reflect changes in business priorities, technology landscape, and industry trends.

In summary, developing a roadmap for AI implementation requires careful planning, stakeholder engagement, and a systematic approach to translating strategic objectives into actionable plans. By following these key steps and best practices, organizations can navigate the complexities of AI adoption, maximize the benefits of AI-driven solutions, and position themselves for long-term success in the increasingly digital and AI-driven economy.

CHAPTER 5

RETAIL INDUSTRY - AI-POWERED PERSONALIZATION

Company: Retail Companies

Overview: Retail Companies, a leading retail chain, implemented an AI-powered personalization strategy to enhance customer engagement, drive sales, and improve overall shopping experiences. By leveraging advanced machine learning algorithms and customer data analytics, Retail Companies aimed to deliver personalized product recommendations, tailored promotions, and targeted marketing campaigns across digital and offline channels.

Implementation:

Retail Companies deployed AI-driven recommendation engines and predictive analytics algorithms to analyze customer behavior, preferences, and purchase history.

93

By integrating data from online transactions, loyalty programs, social media interactions, and in-store purchases, Retail Companies gained insights into customer preferences, trends, and buying patterns.

AI algorithms dynamically generated personalized product recommendations, promotional offers, and content recommendations based on individual customer profiles and real-time interactions.

Results:

Increased Customer Engagement: AI-powered personalization led to a significant increase in customer engagement metrics, including click-through rates, conversion rates, and average order values.

Enhanced Customer Satisfaction: Personalized product recommendations and targeted promotions improved customer satisfaction and loyalty, leading to higher customer retention rates and repeat purchases.

Revenue Growth: AI-driven personalization contributed to a

94

measurable increase in revenue and profitability for Retail Companies, as customers responded positively to relevant and timely offers.

Competitive Advantage: By delivering superior customer experiences through AI-powered personalization, Retail Companies gained a competitive edge in the highly competitive retail landscape.

Lessons Learned:

Data Quality and Integration: Ensuring data quality and integrating data from multiple sources are critical for the success of AI-powered personalization initiatives.

Customer Privacy and Transparency: Maintaining transparency and obtaining consent for data usage are essential to build trust and compliance with privacy regulations.

Continuous Optimization: Continuous monitoring, testing, and optimization of AI algorithms are necessary to adapt to changing customer preferences and market dynamics.

Case Study 2: Healthcare Industry - AI-driven Diagnostics

Company: Health Systems

Overview: Health Systems, a leading healthcare provider, implemented AI-driven diagnostics to improve the accuracy, speed, and efficiency of medical diagnoses. By leveraging machine learning algorithms and medical imaging data, ABC Health Systems aimed to enhance diagnostic accuracy, reduce healthcare costs, and improve patient outcomes across a range of medical specialties.

Implementation:

Health Systems deployed AI-powered diagnostic tools and image recognition algorithms to analyze medical images, including X-rays, MRI scans, and CT scans.

By training AI models on large datasets of labeled medical images, ABC Health Systems enabled automated detection, classification, and analysis of abnormalities and medical conditions.

96

Radiologists and healthcare professionals collaborated with data scientists to develop and validate AI algorithms, ensuring accuracy, reliability, and clinical relevance.

Results:

Improved Diagnostic Accuracy: AI-driven diagnostics led to a significant improvement in diagnostic accuracy and precision, reducing the likelihood of false positives and false negatives.

Faster Turnaround Times: Automated image analysis and diagnosis accelerated the turnaround times for medical imaging reports, enabling faster treatment decisions and improved patient care.

Cost Savings: AI-driven diagnostics reduced healthcare costs associated with unnecessary tests, misdiagnoses, and delayed treatments, resulting in more efficient resource allocation and cost-effective healthcare delivery.

Enhanced Patient Outcomes: By enabling earlier detection and intervention, AI-driven diagnostics improved patient outcomes, reduced morbidity and mortality rates, and enhanced overall quality of care.

Lessons Learned:

Clinical Validation and Expert Oversight: Collaboration between data scientists and healthcare professionals is essential to validate AI algorithms and ensure clinical relevance and accuracy.

Regulatory Compliance: Compliance with regulatory requirements and quality standards is critical for the adoption and integration of AI-driven diagnostics into clinical practice.

Ethical Considerations: Ethical considerations, including patient privacy, informed consent, and transparency in AI-driven diagnostics, must be carefully addressed to uphold patient trust and confidentiality.

In summary, these case studies illustrate how AI-driven technologies can create tangible business value and drive innovation across different industries, from retail to healthcare. By embracing AI as a strategic imperative and leveraging its transformative potential, businesses can unlock new opportunities, improve operational efficiency, and deliver superior customer experiences in the increasingly digital and AI-driven economy.

Success Stories of Businesses Leveraging AI

Netflix: Personalized Content Recommendations:

Netflix, the global streaming giant, leverages AI algorithms to deliver personalized content recommendations to its subscribers.

By analyzing user behavior, viewing history, and preferences, Netflix's recommendation engine suggests relevant movies and TV shows, leading to increased user engagement and retention.

AI-driven personalization has contributed to Netflix's growth and dominance in the highly competitive streaming market, demonstrating the power of AI in enhancing customer experiences and driving business success.

Amazon: Predictive Analytics and Supply Chain Optimization:

Amazon, the e-commerce giant, utilizes AI-powered predictive analytics and supply chain optimization to improve inventory management and fulfillment processes.

By analyzing historical sales data, customer behavior, and market trends, Amazon forecasts demand, anticipates inventory needs, and optimizes product availability across its vast network of warehouses.

AI-driven supply chain optimization enables Amazon to reduce costs, minimize stockouts, and streamline operations, leading to faster deliveries and higher customer satisfaction levels.

Google: Natural Language Processing and Voice Recognition:

Google, the tech giant, harnesses AI technologies such as natural language processing (NLP) and voice recognition to enhance its search engine, virtual assistants, and communication tools.

Google's AI-powered algorithms understand and interpret user queries, extract relevant information from vast amounts of data, and deliver accurate search results in real-time.

Voice-enabled assistants like Google Assistant leverage AI to understand and respond to voice commands, perform tasks, and provide personalized recommendations, revolutionizing the way users interact with technology and access information.

Tesla: Autonomous Driving and AI-enabled Vehicles:

Tesla, the electric car manufacturer, pioneers the development of autonomous driving technology and AI-enabled vehicles.

Tesla's vehicles are equipped with advanced sensors, cameras, and AI algorithms that enable features such as Autopilot, self-driving capabilities, and predictive maintenance.

AI-driven innovations in Tesla's vehicles enhance safety, efficiency, and convenience for drivers, paving the way for a future of autonomous transportation and sustainable mobility solutions.

Zillow: AI-powered Real Estate Insights and Predictive Analytics:

Zillow, the online real estate marketplace, utilizes AI-powered algorithms and predictive analytics to provide real-time property valuations, market insights, and personalized recommendations to homebuyers and sellers.

By analyzing housing market data, property listings, and user preferences, Zillow's AI algorithms generate accurate estimates of property values, identify investment opportunities, and facilitate informed decision-making in real estate transactions.

AI-driven real estate insights empower users to navigate the complexities of the housing market, make confident decisions, and achieve their homeownership goals with greater transparency and efficiency.

In summary, these success stories illustrate how businesses across various industries leverage AI technologies to drive innovation, improve operational efficiency, and enhance customer experiences. By embracing AI as a strategic enabler and investing in AI-driven solutions, businesses can unlock new opportunities, stay ahead of the competition, and thrive in the rapidly evolving digital landscape of the 21st century.

Lessons Learned from Failures and Setbacks in AI Adoption

Insufficient Data Quality and Quantity:

One of the common pitfalls in AI adoption is inadequate data quality and quantity. Businesses may encounter challenges related to incomplete, inaccurate, or biased data, which can undermine the performance and reliability of AI algorithms.

Lesson: Prioritize data quality assurance processes, invest in data governance frameworks, and ensure access to diverse and representative datasets to support robust AI-driven decision-making.

Lack of Alignment with Business Objectives:

AI initiatives that are not closely aligned with business objectives and strategic priorities may fail to deliver meaningful value to the organization. Failure to define clear use cases, establish measurable goals, and secure executive buy-in can result in misalignment and wasted resources.

Lesson: Ensure alignment between AI initiatives and business objectives, involve key stakeholders in the decision-making process, and articulate the expected outcomes and benefits of AI adoption from the outset.

Overreliance on Technology without Human Oversight:

Overreliance on AI technology without human oversight and intervention can lead to unintended consequences, ethical dilemmas, and loss of trust among stakeholders. Blind faith in AI algorithms and automation may overlook critical human judgment, context, and ethical considerations.

Lesson: Maintain human oversight and accountability in AI-driven processes, establish ethical guidelines and frameworks for responsible AI deployment, and foster a culture of transparency, fairness, and accountability within the organization.

Skills Gaps and Talent Shortages:

Many organizations struggle to acquire and retain talent with the necessary expertise in data science, machine learning, and AI technologies. Skills gaps and talent shortages can hinder the successful implementation and scaling of AI initiatives.

Lesson: Invest in talent development and skills acquisition programs, provide training and professional development opportunities for employees, and foster interdisciplinary collaboration between technical and business teams to bridge skills gaps and build AI capabilities within the organization.

105

BUSINESS CASE FOR AI: WHY EVERY BUSINESS NEEDSAN AI STRATEGY

Underestimating Change Management and Organizational Culture:

Underestimating the importance of change management and organizational culture can impede the adoption and acceptance of AI-driven technologies within the organization. Resistance to change, lack of awareness, and cultural barriers may undermine the success of AI initiatives.

Lesson: Prioritize change management efforts, communicate the benefits and rationale behind AI adoption, involve employees in the process of change, and create a supportive and inclusive organizational culture that embraces innovation and continuous learning.

Failure to Address Bias and Fairness in AI Models:

AI algorithms are susceptible to bias and discrimination, which can perpetuate existing inequalities and undermine trust in AI-driven systems. Failure to address bias and fairness in AI models can lead to unintended consequences and negative societal impacts.

Lesson: Implement mechanisms for detecting and mitigating bias in AI models, conduct thorough fairness assessments, involve diverse stakeholders in the development and evaluation of AI algorithms, and prioritize ethical considerations throughout the AI lifecycle.

In summary, learning from failures and setbacks in AI adoption is essential for businesses seeking to build a strong foundation for AI-driven innovation and growth. By recognizing common pitfalls, addressing key challenges, and embracing a culture of continuous improvement, businesses can navigate the complexities of AI adoption, maximize the benefits of AI-driven technologies, and unlock new opportunities for success in the digital age.

Strategies for Overcoming Common Challenges in AI Adoption

Data Quality Assurance:

Strategy: Implement rigorous data quality assurance processes to ensure the accuracy, completeness, and reliability of data used for AI training and decision-making.

Action Steps: Invest in data governance frameworks, establish data quality standards and metrics, conduct data audits and validations, and leverage data cleansing and normalization techniques to improve data quality.

Alignment with Business Objectives:

Strategy: Align AI initiatives closely with business objectives, strategic priorities, and customer needs to ensure meaningful value creation and return on investment.

Action Steps: Engage key stakeholders early in the AI adoption process, define clear use cases and success criteria, conduct thorough business impact assessments, and communicate the strategic rationale and benefits of AI adoption across the organization.

Talent Acquisition and Skills Development:

Strategy: Invest in talent acquisition and skills development programs to build a workforce with the necessary expertise in data science, machine learning, and AI technologies.

Action Steps: Recruit top talent from diverse backgrounds, provide training and professional development opportunities for employees, establish partnerships with academic institutions and industry organizations, and foster a culture of continuous learning and innovation.

Ethical Considerations and Responsible AI Practices:

Strategy: Prioritize ethical considerations and responsible AI practices throughout the AI lifecycle, from data collection and model development to deployment and monitoring.

Action Steps: Establish ethical guidelines and frameworks for AI deployment, conduct thorough risk assessments and impact analyses, promote transparency and accountability in AI-driven decision-making, and engage with stakeholders to address concerns and build trust.

Change Management and Organizational Culture:

Strategy: Prioritize change management efforts and foster a culture of innovation, collaboration, and continuous learning within the organization.

Action Steps: Communicate the vision and benefits of AI adoption, involve employees in the decision-making process, provide training and support for employees transitioning to AI-driven roles, and recognize and reward innovation and experimentation.

Regulatory Compliance and Risk Management:

Strategy: Ensure compliance with regulatory requirements and mitigate risks associated with AI adoption, including data privacy, security, and legal considerations.

Action Steps: Stay informed about relevant regulations and guidelines governing AI deployment, conduct regular compliance audits and assessments, implement robust security measures and data protection protocols, and establish contingency plans and risk mitigation strategies.

Bias Detection and Fairness in AI Models:

Strategy: Implement mechanisms for detecting and mitigating bias in AI models, and prioritize fairness and transparency in AI-driven decision-making.

Action Steps: Conduct bias audits and fairness assessments of AI algorithms, involve diverse stakeholders in the development and evaluation of AI models, monitor and evaluate AI performance for fairness and equity, and address bias through algorithmic adjustments and corrective measures.

Technical Infrastructure and Scalability:

Strategy: Invest in scalable and adaptable technical infrastructure to support AI-driven initiatives and accommodate future growth and expansion.

Action Steps: Evaluate and upgrade existing IT infrastructure, leverage cloud computing and scalable storage solutions, optimize resource allocation and performance tuning, and consider flexible deployment options such as hybrid or multi-cloud environments.

In summary, overcoming common challenges in AI adoption requires a strategic and holistic approach that addresses technical, organizational, regulatory, and ethical considerations. By implementing these strategies and best practices, businesses can navigate the complexities of AI adoption, maximize the benefits of AI-driven technologies, and position themselves for success in the digital age.

CHAPTER 6

RISKS AND MITIGATION STRATEGIES IN AI ADOPTION

Data Privacy and Security Risks

Risk: Data breaches, unauthorized access, and privacy violations pose significant risks when handling sensitive customer data in AI-driven systems.

Mitigation Strategy: Implement robust data encryption, access controls, and authentication mechanisms to protect sensitive information. Adhere to data privacy regulations such as GDPR and CCPA, conduct regular security audits and penetration testing, and invest in cybersecurity training for employees.

Algorithmic Bias and Discrimination:

Risk: AI algorithms may inadvertently perpetuate bias and discrimination, leading to unfair outcomes and negative societal impacts.

Mitigation Strategy: Conduct bias audits and fairness assessments of AI models, prioritize diversity and inclusivity in data collection and model development, implement algorithmic transparency and accountability measures, and involve diverse stakeholders in the design and evaluation of AI systems.

Lack of Transparency and Explainability:

Risk: Opacity and lack of transparency in AI algorithms and decision-making processes can erode trust and accountability.

Mitigation Strategy: Prioritize explainability and interpretability in AI models, employ techniques such as model interpretability, sensitivity analysis, and feature importance ranking, document model assumptions and limitations, and communicate AI-driven decisions in clear and understandable terms to stakeholders.

114

Technical Failures and System Errors:

Risk: Technical failures, system errors, and algorithmic defects can lead to unintended consequences, service disruptions, and financial losses.

Mitigation Strategy: Implement rigorous testing and validation procedures for AI algorithms, monitor system performance and reliability in real-time, establish failover mechanisms and redundancy measures, and develop contingency plans and incident response protocols to mitigate the impact of technical failures.

Dependency on Third-party Vendors and Platforms:

Risk: Dependence on third-party vendors and platforms for AI technologies and services can pose risks related to vendor lock-in, service disruptions, and changes in licensing terms.

Mitigation Strategy: Diversify vendor relationships and maintain flexibility in technology partnerships, conduct thorough vendor assessments and due diligence, negotiate service level agreements (SLAs) and exit clauses, and build in-house expertise to reduce dependency on external vendors.

Regulatory Compliance and Legal Risks:

Risk: Non-compliance with regulatory requirements and legal obligations related to AI deployment can result in fines, legal liabilities, and reputational damage.

Mitigation Strategy: Stay abreast of relevant regulations and guidelines governing AI adoption, establish compliance frameworks and governance structures, conduct regular compliance audits and assessments, and engage legal counsel to review AI-related contracts and agreements.

Ethical Considerations and Social Impacts:

Risk: Ethical dilemmas, social impacts, and unintended consequences of AI adoption can undermine public trust and lead to reputational harm.

Mitigation Strategy: Prioritize ethical considerations and responsible AI practices throughout the AI lifecycle, conduct ethical impact assessments and stakeholder consultations, establish ethical guidelines and codes of conduct for AI deployment, and engage with communities and advocacy groups to address societal concerns.

Skills Gaps and Talent Shortages:

Risk: Shortages of talent with the necessary expertise in data science, machine learning, and AI technologies can hinder the successful implementation and scaling of AI initiatives.

Mitigation Strategy: Invest in talent development and skills acquisition programs, provide training and professional development opportunities for employees, foster interdisciplinary collaboration and knowledge sharing, and leverage external resources such as academic partnerships and industry networks to address skills gaps.

In summary, identifying and mitigating risks associated with AI adoption requires a proactive and multi-faceted approach that addresses technical, organizational,

117

regulatory, ethical, and societal considerations. By implementing robust risk management strategies and best practices, businesses can navigate the complexities of AI adoption, minimize potential liabilities, and maximize the benefits of AI-driven technologies for sustainable growth and innovation.

Data Privacy and Security Concerns in AI Adoption

Data Breaches and Unauthorized Access:

Data breaches and unauthorized access to sensitive information pose significant risks to businesses leveraging AI technologies. Inadequate security measures and vulnerabilities in data storage, transmission, and processing systems can expose confidential data to malicious actors.

Compliance with Data Protection Regulations:

Businesses must comply with data protection regulations such as the General Data Protection Regulation (GDPR) and the California Consumer Privacy Act (CCPA).

Failure to adhere to these regulations can result in hefty fines, legal liabilities, and reputational damage.

Inadequate Data Encryption and Access Controls:

Inadequate data encryption and access controls can leave data vulnerable to interception and exploitation by unauthorized users. Businesses must implement robust encryption mechanisms and access controls to protect sensitive information from unauthorized access and disclosure.

Third-party Data Sharing and Privacy Risks:

Sharing data with third-party vendors and partners can introduce privacy risks and compliance challenges. Businesses must ensure that data sharing agreements and contracts include provisions for data protection, confidentiality, and compliance with regulatory requirements.

Ethical Use of Data and Consumer Trust:

Ethical considerations surrounding the use of consumer data in AI-driven systems are paramount. Businesses must uphold ethical principles, transparency, and accountability in data collection, usage, and processing to maintain consumer trust and confidence.

Algorithmic Bias and Discrimination:

Algorithmic bias and discrimination can result in unfair treatment and disparate impacts on individuals and groups. Businesses must mitigate bias in AI algorithms by implementing fairness-aware techniques, diversity in data representation, and ongoing monitoring and evaluation.

Data Localization and Cross-border Data Transfers:

Data localization requirements and restrictions on cross-border data transfers can pose challenges for businesses operating in multiple jurisdictions. Businesses must navigate complex legal and regulatory landscapes to ensure compliance with data sovereignty and localization requirements.

Vendor and Supply Chain Security Risks:

Businesses must assess and mitigate security risks associated with third-party vendors and supply chain partners. Weaknesses in vendor security practices and supply chain vulnerabilities can expose businesses to data breaches, cyberattacks, and supply chain disruptions.

Insider Threats and Employee Misuse:

Insider threats and employee misuse of data pose internal security risks to businesses. Employing robust access controls, monitoring systems, and employee training programs can help mitigate the risk of insider threats and unauthorized data access.

Emerging Threats and Cybersecurity Risks:

Businesses must stay vigilant against emerging threats and cybersecurity risks in the evolving landscape of AI-driven technologies. Proactive threat intelligence, vulnerability assessments, and incident response capabilities are essential for safeguarding against cyber threats and data breaches.

In summary, addressing data privacy and security concerns is critical for businesses implementing AI strategies. By implementing robust security measures, adhering to data protection regulations, and upholding ethical principles, businesses can mitigate risks, build consumer trust, and unlock the full potential of AI-driven technologies in the digital age.

Bias and Fairness Issues in AI Algorithms

Introduction to Bias in AI Algorithms:

Bias in AI algorithms refers to the systematic and unfair preferences or prejudices encoded in the data or design of the algorithm, leading to discriminatory outcomes or unequal treatment of individuals or groups.

Types of Bias in AI Algorithms:

Sampling Bias: Occurs when the training data used to develop AI models is not representative of the population it seeks to serve, leading to skewed or incomplete representations of certain demographic groups.

Selection Bias: Arises when certain attributes or characteristics are overrepresented or underrepresented in the training data, leading to biased predictions or classifications.

Algorithmic Bias: Occurs due to inherent limitations or assumptions in the algorithm design, leading to systematic errors or disparities in decision-making.

Historical Bias: Reflects the historical inequalities and biases present in society that may be perpetuated or amplified by AI algorithms trained on historical data.

Impact of Bias in AI Algorithms:

Bias in AI algorithms can have far-reaching consequences, including:

Reinforcing and exacerbating existing inequalities and disparities in society.

Discriminatory treatment and unfair outcomes for individuals or groups based on protected characteristics such as race, gender, ethnicity, or socioeconomic status.

Undermining trust and credibility in AI-driven systems and eroding public confidence in technology.

Examples of Bias in AI Algorithms:

Facial Recognition: Facial recognition algorithms have been shown to exhibit higher error rates for individuals with darker skin tones, leading to disparities in accuracy and misidentification.

Recidivism Prediction: Predictive policing algorithms used to assess recidivism risk have been found to disproportionately target and penalize minority communities, reflecting biases present in historical arrest and incarceration data.

Employment Screening: AI-based hiring tools may inadvertently perpetuate gender or racial biases in recruitment processes, leading to discriminatory outcomes and exclusionary practices.

Mitigation Strategies for Bias in AI Algorithms:

Data Collection and Preprocessing: Ensure diversity and representativeness in training data, identify and mitigate biases in data collection and preprocessing stages.

Algorithmic Transparency: Enhance transparency and explainability of AI algorithms to enable stakeholders to understand and interpret model decisions.

Fairness-aware Algorithms: Develop fairness-aware algorithms that explicitly account for fairness constraints and considerations during model training and evaluation.

Diverse and Inclusive Teams: Foster diversity and inclusion in AI development teams to bring diverse perspectives and mitigate biases in algorithm design and decision-making processes.

Continuous Monitoring and Evaluation: Implement mechanisms for continuous monitoring and evaluation of AI algorithms to detect and address bias over time, conduct regular audits and

125

assessments of model fairness and performance.

In summary, addressing bias and fairness issues in AI algorithms is essential for building ethical, equitable, and responsible AI systems. By recognizing the complexities of bias in AI algorithms and implementing robust mitigation strategies, businesses can uphold ethical principles, promote fairness and inclusivity, and mitigate risks associated with biased decision-making in AI-driven technologies.

Strategies for Mitigating Risks and Building Trust in AI Adoption

Transparency and Explainability:

Strategy: Prioritize transparency and explainability in AI systems to foster understanding and trust among stakeholders.

Action Steps: Provide clear explanations of AI algorithms and decision-making processes, disclose data sources and model assumptions, and offer insights into how AI-driven decisions are made.

126

Ethical Guidelines and Responsible AI Practices:

Strategy: Establish ethical guidelines and responsible AI practices to guide the development, deployment, and use of AI technologies.

Action Steps: Develop and communicate ethical principles for AI adoption, prioritize fairness, accountability, and transparency in AI-driven decision-making, and adhere to industry standards and best practices.

Fairness-aware Algorithms and Bias Mitigation:

Strategy: Develop fairness-aware algorithms and implement bias mitigation techniques to ensure equitable outcomes and mitigate discriminatory impacts.

Action Steps: Conduct bias audits and fairness assessments of AI algorithms, implement algorithmic adjustments and corrective measures to address bias, and prioritize diversity and inclusivity in data collection and model development.

Data Privacy and Security Measures:

Strategy: Implement robust data privacy and security measures to protect sensitive information and mitigate the risk of data breaches and unauthorized access.

Action Steps: Encrypt data at rest and in transit, implement access controls and authentication mechanisms, conduct regular security audits and vulnerability assessments, and comply with data protection regulations and privacy laws.

Stakeholder Engagement and Collaboration:

Strategy: Foster stakeholder engagement and collaboration to build consensus, address concerns, and promote transparency in AI adoption.

Action Steps: Engage with customers, employees, regulators, and communities to solicit feedback and input, involve stakeholders in the decision-making process, and communicate openly and transparently about AI initiatives.

Risk Management and Contingency Planning:

Strategy: Implement risk management practices and develop contingency plans to mitigate potential risks and respond effectively to unforeseen challenges.

Action Steps: Identify and assess potential risks associated with AI adoption, develop risk mitigation strategies and controls, establish contingency plans and incident response protocols, and monitor and evaluate risks on an ongoing basis.

Education and Training Programs:

Strategy: Provide education and training programs to enhance AI literacy and empower stakeholders to make informed decisions about AI technologies.

Action Steps: Offer training sessions, workshops, and resources to educate employees and stakeholders about AI concepts, benefits, and risks, promote digital literacy and critical thinking skills, and raise awareness about responsible AI practices.

Accountability and Governance Frameworks:

Strategy: Establish accountability mechanisms and governance frameworks to ensure responsible AI deployment and oversight.

Action Steps: Define roles and responsibilities for AI governance and oversight, establish clear accountability structures and decision-making processes, and implement mechanisms for monitoring and evaluating AI performance and compliance with ethical and regulatory standards.

In summary, mitigating risks and building trust in AI adoption requires a proactive and multi-faceted approach that addresses technical, organizational, regulatory, and ethical considerations. By implementing these strategies and best practices, businesses can foster trust, promote transparency, and maximize the benefits of AI-driven technologies in the digital age.

CHAPTER 7

FUTURE TRENDS AND PREDICTIONS IN AI

Advancements in Natural Language Processing (NLP)

Future AI systems will exhibit improved capabilities in understanding and generating human language, leading to more natural and intuitive interactions between humans and machines. NLP technologies will enable advancements in virtual assistants, chatbots, language translation, and sentiment analysis.

Explainable AI (XAI):

There will be a growing emphasis on developing explainable AI (XAI) systems that provide transparent explanations of AI-driven decisions and recommendations. XAI technologies will enhance trust, accountability, and understanding of AI algorithms, particularly in high-stakes applications such as healthcare and finance.

131

AI-powered Automation and Robotics:

Automation and robotics will be increasingly powered by AI technologies, leading to the proliferation of intelligent systems and autonomous agents in various industries. AI-driven automation will transform manufacturing, logistics, transportation, and service sectors, improving efficiency, productivity, and safety.

Edge Computing and AI at the Edge:

Edge computing will enable AI processing and inference to occur closer to the source of data generation, reducing latency, bandwidth requirements, and dependence on centralized cloud infrastructure. AI at the edge will empower IoT devices, smart sensors, and autonomous vehicles to make real-time decisions and respond to dynamic environments.

Ethical AI and Responsible Innovation:

There will be increasing emphasis on ethical AI and responsible innovation practices to address societal concerns, mitigate bias and discrimination, and uphold human rights and dignity. Businesses will adopt ethical guidelines, fairness-aware algorithms, and governance frameworks to ensure the responsible deployment of AI technologies.

AI-enabled Personalization and Hyper-personalization:

AI-driven personalization will evolve towards hyper-personalization, delivering highly tailored and contextually relevant experiences to individual users. AI algorithms will analyze vast amounts of data to anticipate user preferences, behavior patterns, and intent, enabling personalized recommendations, content, and services across digital and physical channels.

AI in Healthcare and Precision Medicine:

AI will revolutionize healthcare and precision medicine, enabling more accurate diagnostics, personalized treatments, and proactive disease prevention strategies. AI algorithms will analyze medical imaging data, genomic sequences, electronic health records, and patient data to accelerate medical research, improve clinical outcomes, and enhance patient care.

AI-driven Innovation in Renewable Energy and Sustainability:

AI technologies will drive innovation in renewable energy, sustainability, and environmental conservation efforts. AI algorithms will optimize energy consumption, manage grid systems, and enhance resource efficiency in energy production and distribution, contributing to the transition towards a greener and more sustainable future.

AI Governance and Regulation:

There will be increased scrutiny and regulation of AI technologies to address concerns related to privacy, security, fairness, and accountability. Governments and regulatory bodies will develop policies, standards, and guidelines to ensure the responsible and ethical use of AI, while balancing innovation and economic growth.

Collaborative AI and Human-AI Collaboration:

Collaboration between humans and AI systems will become more seamless and intuitive, with AI acting as augmentative tools to enhance human capabilities and decision-making processes. Human-AI collaboration will empower individuals, teams, and organizations to solve complex problems, drive innovation, and achieve transformative outcomes.

Emerging Technologies Shaping the Future of AI

Quantum Computing:

Quantum computing holds the potential to revolutionize AI by exponentially increasing computing power and enabling more complex calculations and simulations. Quantum algorithms could accelerate AI training processes, optimize resource allocation, and solve previously intractable problems in areas such as cryptography, optimization, and drug discovery.

Neuromorphic Computing:

Neuromorphic computing architectures mimic the structure and functionality of the human brain, enabling AI systems to process information in a more efficient and biomimetic manner. Neuromorphic chips and hardware accelerate AI inference tasks, support real-time processing, and enable energy-efficient computing for edge devices and IoT applications.

Federated Learning:

Federated learning is a decentralized approach to AI training that allows models to be trained across distributed devices and edge nodes without centralizing data. Federated learning enables privacy-preserving AI training, reduces communication overhead, and fosters collaboration among decentralized participants while maintaining data locality and privacy.

Generative Adversarial Networks (GANs):

GANs are a class of AI algorithms that generate synthetic data by pitting two neural networks against each other in a competitive process. GANs have applications in image synthesis, text generation, and creative design, enabling AI systems to produce realistic and diverse

136

outputs that mimic human creativity and imagination.

Explainable AI (XAI):

Explainable AI (XAI) techniques enable AI systems to provide transparent explanations of their decisions and recommendations, enhancing trust, accountability, and interpretability. XAI methods such as attention mechanisms, saliency maps, and feature attribution techniques enable users to understand and interpret AI-driven decisions, particularly in critical domains such as healthcare and finance.

Robotics and Autonomous Systems:

Robotics and autonomous systems leverage AI technologies such as computer vision, sensor fusion, and reinforcement learning to enable robots and autonomous vehicles to perceive, navigate, and interact with their environments autonomously. AI-powered robotics have applications in manufacturing, logistics, healthcare, and transportation, enabling automation, efficiency, and safety.

137

Edge AI and Edge Computing:

Edge AI brings AI processing and inference capabilities closer to the source of data generation, enabling real-time decision-making, low-latency responses, and reduced dependence on centralized cloud infrastructure. Edge AI technologies enable AI inference tasks to be performed directly on edge devices, sensors, and IoT endpoints, enabling intelligent edge computing solutions.

Biologically Inspired AI:

Biologically inspired AI draws inspiration from principles of biology, neuroscience, and cognitive science to develop AI algorithms and systems that emulate biological intelligence and behavior. Biologically inspired AI techniques such as spiking neural networks, evolutionary algorithms, and swarm intelligence enable AI systems to adapt, learn, and evolve in dynamic environments.

AI Chips and Hardware Accelerators:

AI chips and hardware accelerators are specialized semiconductor devices optimized for AI workloads, including

138

training and inference tasks. AI-specific chips such as graphics processing units (GPUs), tensor processing units (TPUs), and neuromorphic processors enable faster computation, lower power consumption, and higher efficiency for AI-driven applications.

Blockchain and AI Integration:

Blockchain technology and AI integration enable secure, transparent, and decentralized AI applications, facilitating data sharing, collaboration, and trust among multiple parties. Blockchain-based AI solutions enable data provenance, auditability, and integrity verification, enhancing trust and accountability in AI-driven ecosystems.

Potential Impacts of AI on Industries and Society

Increased Efficiency and Productivity:

AI technologies have the potential to streamline processes, automate repetitive tasks, and optimize resource allocation across industries. By leveraging AI-driven automation and optimization, businesses can enhance efficiency, reduce operational costs, and improve productivity.

Innovation and New Business Models:

AI enables businesses to innovate and develop new products, services, and business models that were previously unattainable. From personalized recommendations to predictive analytics, AI-driven innovations have the potential to disrupt traditional industries and create new opportunities for growth and differentiation.

Enhanced Decision-making and Insights:

AI-powered analytics and decision support systems provide businesses with actionable insights, predictive analytics, and data-driven recommendations to inform strategic decision-making. By harnessing the power of AI-driven analytics, businesses can gain a competitive edge, identify market trends, and capitalize on emerging opportunities.

Personalization and Customer Experience:

AI enables personalized and contextually relevant experiences for customers across industries, from e-commerce and retail to healthcare and finance. By analyzing vast amounts of data and leveraging machine learning algorithms, businesses can tailor products, services, and marketing messages to individual preferences and behavior patterns.

Improved Healthcare and Patient Outcomes:

AI technologies hold the potential to revolutionize healthcare delivery, diagnosis, and treatment, enabling more accurate diagnostics, personalized medicine, and proactive disease prevention strategies. AI-driven medical imaging, predictive analytics, and clinical decision support systems can improve patient outcomes, reduce medical errors, and enhance the quality and efficiency of healthcare services.

Transformed Transportation and Mobility:

AI-powered technologies such as autonomous vehicles, ride-sharing platforms, and traffic management systems are transforming the transportation and mobility landscape. AI enables safer, more efficient, and sustainable transportation solutions, reducing traffic congestion, emissions, and accidents while improving mobility access and convenience for individuals and communities.

Ethical and Societal Implications:

The widespread adoption of AI raises ethical, social, and policy considerations related to privacy, security, bias, accountability, and employment. Businesses and policymakers must address these ethical and societal implications to ensure responsible AI deployment and mitigate potential risks and negative impacts on individuals and communities.

Workforce Transformation and Skills Development:

AI-driven automation and augmentation are reshaping the nature of work and requiring individuals to adapt and acquire new skills. While AI technologies have the potential to enhance productivity and create new job opportunities, they also pose challenges related to job displacement, skills gaps, and workforce reskilling and upskilling.

Environmental Sustainability and Conservation:

AI technologies can contribute to environmental sustainability and conservation efforts by optimizing resource usage, mitigating environmental risks, and enabling more efficient energy management and conservation practices. From precision agriculture to smart energy grids, AI-driven solutions have the potential to address environmental challenges and promote sustainable development.

Global Economic Competitiveness and Growth:

AI is driving global economic competitiveness and growth by fostering

143

innovation, entrepreneurship, and technological advancement across industries and sectors. Countries and businesses that invest in AI research, development, and adoption are better positioned to compete in the digital economy and seize opportunities for economic prosperity and societal progress.

Strategies for Staying Ahead in the AI-Driven Economy

Invest in AI Research and Development:

Allocate resources and investments towards AI research and development to stay at the forefront of technological innovation. Foster collaboration with academic institutions, research labs, and industry partners to drive advancements in AI algorithms, methodologies, and applications.

Build AI Talent and Expertise:

Develop a skilled workforce with expertise in data science, machine learning, and AI technologies. Invest in talent acquisition, training programs, and professional development initiatives to build a diverse and multidisciplinary team capable of leveraging AI for innovation and growth.

Embrace Continuous Learning and Adaptation:

Foster a culture of continuous learning, experimentation, and adaptation to keep pace with evolving AI technologies and market dynamics. Encourage employees to explore new ideas, acquire new skills, and embrace emerging trends in AI-driven innovation and entrepreneurship.

Forge Strategic Partnerships and Alliances:

Establish strategic partnerships and alliances with technology vendors, startups, research institutions, and industry consortia to access cutting-edge AI technologies, insights, and resources. Collaborate with ecosystem partners to co-create innovative solutions, leverage complementary capabilities, and drive collective impact in the AI-driven economy.

Prioritize Customer-Centric Innovation:

Put customers at the center of innovation efforts and focus on addressing their

145

evolving needs, preferences, and pain points. Leverage AI-driven analytics, customer insights, and feedback mechanisms to anticipate trends, personalize experiences, and deliver value-added solutions that resonate with customers.

Develop Agile and Adaptive Business Models:

Embrace agility and adaptability in business models to respond quickly to market changes, competitive pressures, and technological disruptions. Experiment with new business models, revenue streams, and go-to-market strategies that leverage AI technologies to create differentiated value propositions and sustainable competitive advantage.

Drive Data-Driven Decision Making:

Cultivate a data-driven culture and institutionalize data-driven decision-making processes across the organization. Leverage AI-driven analytics, predictive modeling, and business intelligence tools to extract actionable insights, optimize operations, and drive strategic initiatives based on empirical evidence and quantitative analysis.

Mitigate Risks and Ensure Responsible AI Deployment:

Prioritize ethical considerations, fairness, transparency, and accountability in AI deployment to mitigate risks and build trust among stakeholders. Implement robust governance frameworks, ethical guidelines, and risk management practices to ensure responsible AI adoption and adherence to regulatory requirements.

Stay Abreast of Regulatory and Policy Developments:

Monitor regulatory and policy developments related to AI governance, data privacy, cybersecurity, and intellectual property rights to ensure compliance and mitigate legal risks. Engage with policymakers, industry associations, and regulatory authorities to shape policy discussions and advocate for policies that foster innovation while safeguarding societal interests.

Promote Diversity, Inclusion, and Equity:

Foster diversity, inclusion, and equity in AI development, deployment, and usage to mitigate bias, promote fairness, and enhance societal well-being. Embrace diverse perspectives, voices, and talents to build AI systems that reflect the values, needs, and aspirations of diverse communities and stakeholders.

CHAPTER 8

CONCLUSION

In the dynamic landscape of the modern business world, the integration of artificial intelligence (AI) has emerged as a transformative force, reshaping industries, driving innovation, and redefining the ways in which businesses operate and compete. Through the exploration of the business case for AI, it becomes evident that every organization, regardless of its size or industry, needs a well-defined AI strategy to thrive in the digital age.

The journey through the pages of this book has illuminated the myriad opportunities and challenges presented by AI adoption. From enhancing efficiency and productivity to fostering innovation and competitive advantage, AI offers businesses unprecedented capabilities to unlock value, drive growth, and create sustainable impact. Yet, amidst the promises of AI-driven transformation, there are also ethical considerations, societal implications, and risks that demand careful attention and responsible stewardship.

As businesses embark on their AI journey, it is essential to recognize that success requires more than just technological prowess. It necessitates a strategic mindset, a commitment to ethical principles, and a culture of continuous learning and adaptation. By prioritizing transparency, fairness, and accountability in AI deployment, businesses can build trust, mitigate risks, and foster positive relationships with customers, employees, and stakeholders.

Moreover, the imperative for AI strategy extends beyond individual organizations to encompass broader societal and global considerations. As AI becomes increasingly intertwined with the fabric of society, it is incumbent upon policymakers, regulators, and industry leaders to collaborate, innovate, and address the complex challenges and opportunities presented by AI-driven technologies.

Looking ahead, the future of AI holds immense promise and potential to drive inclusive growth, empower individuals, and address some of the most pressing challenges facing humanity. By harnessing the transformative power of AI with

150

foresight, integrity, and purpose, businesses can chart a course towards a more prosperous, equitable, and sustainable future.

In closing, the business case for AI is clear: every business needs an AI strategy to navigate the complexities of the digital age, seize opportunities for innovation, and create value for society. As we embark on this journey together, let us embrace the transformative potential of AI with humility, responsibility, and a shared commitment to shaping a better world for generations to come.

Final Thoughts on the Transformative Power of AI in Business

As we conclude our exploration of the business case for AI, it becomes evident that we stand at the precipice of a profound transformation in the way businesses operate, innovate, and create value in the digital age. The transformative power of AI transcends mere technological advancements; it embodies a paradigm shift that has the potential to reshape

151

industries, redefine business models, and revolutionize the way we work and live.

At its core, the transformative power of AI lies in its ability to augment human intelligence, amplify organizational capabilities, and unlock new frontiers of innovation and growth. From automating repetitive tasks to uncovering hidden insights within vast datasets, AI empowers businesses to operate with unprecedented speed, precision, and scale, thereby enabling them to stay ahead in an increasingly competitive and dynamic marketplace.

Moreover, the transformative impact of AI extends far beyond the confines of individual organizations; it has the potential to drive systemic change, foster economic prosperity, and address some of the most pressing challenges facing society. From improving healthcare outcomes to enhancing environmental sustainability, AI offers solutions to complex problems that were once thought insurmountable, paving the way for a brighter and more inclusive future for all.

Yet, amidst the promises of AI-driven transformation, it is imperative to approach its adoption with a sense of responsibility, foresight, and ethical integrity. As we harness the transformative power of AI, we must remain vigilant against the risks of bias, discrimination, and unintended consequences that may arise. By prioritizing fairness, transparency, and accountability in AI deployment, we can ensure that its benefits are equitably distributed and that its potential to drive positive change is realized to its fullest extent.

In the final analysis, the transformative power of AI in business is not merely a technological phenomenon; it is a reflection of our collective aspirations, ingenuity, and capacity for innovation. As we embark on this journey of discovery and exploration, let us embrace the transformative potential of AI with humility, courage, and a steadfast commitment to shaping a future that is both prosperous and equitable for all.

In the grand tapestry of human progress, AI represents not just a tool or a technology, but a beacon of hope and possibility—a catalyst for unlocking human potential and creating a world that is more connected, more intelligent, and more compassionate than ever before. As we look to the horizon of possibilities that AI affords, let us do so with a sense of wonder, curiosity, and purpose, knowing that the journey ahead is filled with boundless opportunities for growth, discovery, and collective advancement.

In the end, the business case for AI is not just about driving profits or gaining a competitive edge; it is about harnessing the transformative power of technology to build a future that is brighter, more inclusive, and more resilient than we could ever imagine. As we stand on the threshold of this new era of possibility, let us embrace the transformative power of AI with optimism, resolve, and a shared commitment to realizing its full potential for the betterment of humanity and the world we share.

Call to Action

Now is the time for businesses to seize the transformative potential of artificial intelligence (AI) and chart a course towards a future of innovation, growth, and competitive advantage. As we have explored in the pages of "Business Case for

154

AI: Why Every Business Needs an AI Strategy," the imperative for AI strategy has never been clearer nor more pressing.

The call to action is clear: businesses must develop comprehensive AI strategies that align with their vision, goals, and values. Here's how:

Define Your AI Vision and Objectives:

Start by articulating a clear vision for how AI can drive value and contribute to your organization's success. Identify specific objectives, challenges, and opportunities that AI can address across various functions and processes.

Assess Your AI Readiness and Capabilities:

Conduct a thorough assessment of your organization's AI readiness, including technical infrastructure, data assets, talent pool, and organizational culture. Identify gaps, challenges, and opportunities for AI adoption and development.

Invest in Talent and Expertise:

Build a skilled and diverse workforce with expertise in data science, machine learning, and AI technologies. Invest in talent acquisition, training programs, and professional development initiatives to cultivate a culture of innovation and excellence in AI.

Foster a Culture of Experimentation and Innovation:

Foster a culture of experimentation, curiosity, and innovation that encourages employees to explore new ideas, embrace failure as a learning opportunity, and push the boundaries of what is possible with AI.

Prioritize Ethical Considerations and Responsible AI Practices:

Prioritize ethical considerations, fairness, transparency, and accountability in AI deployment and development. Implement robust governance frameworks, ethical guidelines, and risk management practices to ensure responsible AI adoption and deployment.

Forge Strategic Partnerships and Collaborations:

Establish strategic partnerships and collaborations with technology vendors, startups, research institutions, and industry consortia to access cutting-edge AI technologies, insights, and resources. Collaborate with ecosystem partners to co-create innovative solutions and drive collective impact.

Drive Data-Driven Decision Making:

Cultivate a data-driven culture and institutionalize data-driven decision-making processes across the organization. Leverage AI-driven analytics, predictive modeling, and business intelligence tools to extract actionable insights and optimize operations.

Stay Abreast of Emerging Trends and Technologies:

Stay informed and stay ahead of emerging trends, advancements, and innovations in the field of AI. Invest in continuous learning, research, and experimentation to adapt to evolving market dynamics and technological landscapes.

Advocate for Policy and Regulatory Frameworks:

Advocate for policy and regulatory frameworks that foster innovation, safeguard consumer rights, and promote responsible AI deployment. Engage with policymakers, industry associations, and regulatory authorities to shape policy discussions and advocate for policies that balance innovation and accountability.

Lead with Vision, Courage, and Purpose:

Lead with vision, courage, and purpose, knowing that the journey towards AI-driven transformation is one of immense promise, potential, and possibility. Embrace the challenges, embrace the opportunities, and embrace the transformative power of AI to create a future that is brighter, more inclusive, and more prosperous for all.

In conclusion, the business case for AI is compelling, and the time to act is now. By developing comprehensive AI strategies and embracing the transformative power of

AI, businesses can unlock new opportunities for innovation, growth, and societal impact in the digital age. Let us rise to the challenge, let us seize the opportunity, and let us shape a future that is defined by the limitless possibilities of AI-driven innovation and progress.

www.ingramcontent.com/pod-product-compliance
Lightning Source LLC
Chambersburg PA
CBHW071044290526
45795CB00004B/1304